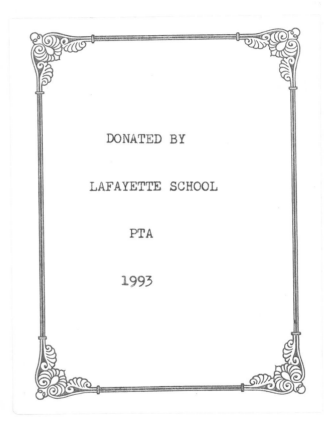

DONATED BY

LAFAYETTE SCHOOL

PTA

1993

# Peregrine Falcon

Published simultaneously in the United
States by Firefly Books (U.S.) Inc. P.O.
Box 1338, Ellicott Station, Buffalo, N.Y.
14205.

ISBN 0-920775-99-3

Printed in Canada on recycled paper

A B C D E F

For permission to use copyrighted photos
we thank: Frans Lanting/Minden Pictures,
pp.4/5, 27; Stephen J. Krasemann/DRK
Photo, p.11; Brian Parker/Tom Stack &
Assoc., pp.12/13, 31;P. McLain/VIREO,
p.16; Wendy Shattil/Bob Rozinski/Tom
Stack & Assoc., p.17; Tom
Brakefield/Bruce Coleman Inc., pp.18/19;
Thomas Kitchin, p.19; Francisco
Erize/Bruce Coleman Inc., pp.20/21;
Animals Animals/Ron Willocks, p.24;
Animals Animals/Breck P. Kent, p.25;
Fred J. Alsop/Bruce Coleman Inc., p.26;
Jeff Foott, p.28; Robert Galbraith/Valan,
p.29; Roy Morsch/Bruce Coleman Inc.,
p.29; F.K. Schleicher/VIREO, pp.30/31.

We are grateful to Dr. Ian Ritchie, Raptor
Research Centre, McGill University, for
his assistance in the preparation of this
book.

Design by Word & Image Design Studio,
Toronto

Silhouette illustrations by Dave McKay

Research by Katherine Farris

Cover photo by Stephen J.
Krasemann/DRK Photo

# Peregrine Falcon

## From OWL Magazine

• • • • • • •

Written by Sylvia Funston
Illustrated by Olena Kassian

OWL

**Greey de Pencier Books**

# Introduction

Scientists describe certain animals as endangered to warn people that, unless we take special care, they will disappear forever from the world.

Many animals are endangered because people have taken over their wilderness homes. Others become endangered because they are over-hunted. Still others are endangered because pollution is poisoning them.

In this book you will discover how peregrine falcons live. You will explore the special reasons they are endangered and find out what is being done — as well as what you can do — to help them survive far into the future.

Falcon...

# QUIZ

Are you up on your falcon facts? Find out with this fast quiz. *Answers page 32*

**1.** A female peregrine falcon is bigger than her mate, but is she the size of:
**a.** a sparrow
**b.** a crow
**c.** an ostrich?

**2.** To entice his mate to check out a nest site, what does a male falcon leave there for her?
**a.** shiny stones
**b.** feathers
**c.** food

**3.** How many eggs does a peregrine falcon lay? Hint: She lays an egg every other day for one week.
**a.** 1
**b.** 4
**c.** 7

**4.** A peregrine chick that has left the nest is called:
**a.** a fledgling
**b.** a featherling
**c.** a starling.

**5.** A peregrine falcon usually stuns its prey in mid air by hitting it with:
**a.** its head
**b.** its feet
**c.** its chest.

**6.** What does the word "peregrine" mean?
**a.** a pair of green eyes
**b.** bird with a grin
**c.** a wanderer

**7.** Before a peregrine falcon brings prey to the nest, it:
**a.** washes the bird in a stream
**b.** flies to a nearby perch and plucks the bird's feathers
**c.** stores the bird for a few days to make it tender.

# Will You Be Mine?

Peregrine falcons mate for life, but usually they spend each winter apart. When they get together again in the spring, the male woos his mate as if they were meeting for the first time. During the courtship, the male shows off his flying skills.

He also brings his mate gifts of food, even feeding her in mid air. Afterwards, they might preen each other's feathers, nibble on a few toes, play chasing games or spend some time scraping in the dirt or bowing and clucking to each other.

In quiet moments, they snuggle together in their nest. One of them often sits with its head upside down so that it can gently peck the other bird.

Peregrines that live in cities stay together all year.

# Baby Peregrines

Stubby pink toes, unseeing eyes and straggly strands of down make this newly-hatched peregrine falcon look quite helpless. But soon it will dry out and turn into a fluffy, warm bundle of silky, soft down.

By the time it is 10 days old, the chick is fully alert. For the first three weeks its mother keeps it safe and warm, while its father supplies the family with food. When he gets tired, the mother hunts.

As new feathers grow, peregrine chicks look like pin cushions.

Fluffy down helps young falcons stay warm, but they need different kinds of feathers to fly. Over the next few weeks these chicks' soft down will be replaced by sleek, brown feathers.

# Growing Up

**W**hat a funny sight this half-grown peregrine looks in its patchwork coat and fluffy down pants. Each day now it exercises its growing wings and plays hunting games with its nest mates.

At last it is time to fly. Peering nervously over the cliff edge, the young bird flaps its wings. The rising air current pushes against them, and in one heart-stopping leap, the youngster soars into the clear, blue sky.

For several weeks the young bird watches its parents hunt. Sometimes one parent drops a dead bird for the youngster to catch in mid air. The other parent swoops low, ready to snatch it up if the young peregrine misses it.

Young peregrines keep their speckled feathers for two years.

# The Hunter

A circling peregrine suddenly folds its wings, tucks in its feet and dives. Far below, it has spotted a flying duck. The peregrine dives so fast that if it grabbed the duck out of the air with its talons it would break its own legs. Instead, the hunter hits its prey with its strongly muscled chest.

The duck falls, unconscious, and the peregrine climbs steeply to slow down. Then it turns and swoops, brakes with its wings and tail, and catches its prey in mid air. The duck is too heavy to carry to a plucking perch, so the peregrine flies down to the ground with it. There, with one swift blow from its sharply notched beak, the peregrine kills the duck.

# The Fastest Hunter on Earth

Something has caught the sharp eye of this adult peregrine falcon. From a height of 1 kilometre (about 1,000 yards) it has spotted a pigeon sitting on the ground.

As soon as the pigeon takes to the air, the falcon will go into a high speed dive, or "stoop." The speed of the attacking falcon, at more than 300 km/h (186 mph), is enough to kill the pigeon on contact.

If a pigeon sees a falcon coming, it can often escape.

17

# Peregrine Falcons Are Amazing

- ► A pilot was flying at 280 km/h (173 mph) in his small plane when, to his surprise, an even faster peregrine falcon flew past him!

- ► Sometimes a chick gets blown off its cliff-side nest before it can fly. If it lands unharmed on a ledge below, its mother will continue to feed it by dropping food down to it.

- ► If they get too close to a peregrine's nest, trespassing birds will soon find themselves in mid-air battle with the peregrine. One fight lasted three hours!

- Peregrine falcons sometimes dive-bomb pigeons without touching them. Are the falcons practising their hunting techniques, or just having fun?

- A peregrine's eyesight is six times sharper than yours! In one experiment, a peregrine recognized a white handkerchief signal from 1.5 km (almost 1 mile) away.

Peregrine falcons like to take a bath every day.

# Where Do Peregrine Falcons Live?

Each spring peregrine falcons nest on narrow ledges high up on sheer cliffs. Their nests are simple hollows scraped out of the soil or gravel. In cities, peregrines nest on ledges on tall buildings.

Peregrines nest high above the trees to protect their young from raccoons, owls and hawks.

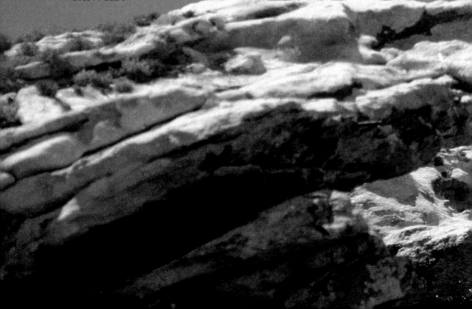

Summary
- Summer range
- Year-round range
- Winter range

In fall, North America's peregrines head south for the winter, some as far as South America. They follow the flocks of songbirds and waterbirds on which they feed. Some, however, remain in large cities where there is a year-round supply of small birds.

# The Peregrine
# Up Close

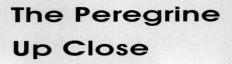

▶ By fanning out its tail
or tightly folding it, the
peregrine can use it either
to slow down or to keep
steady during a dive.

▶ The peregrine also brakes by
spreading its wing feathers,
including a feathered
"thumb" that it can stick
up on the front edge
of each wing.

► A smooth, streamlined shape allows the peregrine to slice through the air in its high-speed dives.

► Its amazing eyesight allows the peregrine to hunt in the dim light of dawn and dusk when its prey is most active.

► By absorbing light and reducing glare, the black stripe beneath the peregrine's eyes helps it to see better. Football players have learned this trick.

# Why Are Peregrine Falcons Endangered?

## Poison and Peregrines

By the early 1970s North America's peregrine falcons were in trouble. The shells on their eggs were so thin that they crushed beneath the weight of the parent birds. The cause was the pesticide DDT. Every time a peregrine ate a bird that had eaten insects or plants containing this chemical, it too got a dose of DDT.

## People and Peregrines

People have forced
peregrines out of their
natural home ranges by
taking over wilderness
for cities, roads and
farmland. They have
disturbed them by
climbing cliffs when they
are nesting. And they
have stopped them
raising their young by
collecting their eggs.

What DDT did to peregrine falcons
forced many people to pay more
attention to the environment.

25

# What's Being Done?

In 1970, a Canadian biologist called Richard Fyfe collected 12 peregrines and made nesting sites for them on his Alberta farm. Fyfe's plan was to save peregrines by tricking them into laying more eggs than they could in the wild. If eggs are removed from the nest as soon as they are laid, a female peregrine goes on laying — as many as 15 eggs! Hatched in an incubator, the extra chicks are cared for by humans.

Wild peregrines raise no more than four chicks.

Hand-raised chick gets a meal from "mom."

The Canadian government liked Fyfe's idea and built homes for 100 peregrines at Camp Wainwright, Alberta. At the same time, the Canadian and American governments banned the use of the pesticides DDT and DDE.

Since then, hundreds of Wainwright peregrines have been released, many in major cities.

# Back to the Wilderness

Some peregrine chicks that are hatched by humans are taken to wilderness cliffs and housed in cages called hack boxes. Two biologists drop food into the box until the birds can hunt.

Other chicks are slipped into the nests of wild peregrines that are raising less than four young. All the chicks must be the same age, less than four weeks old, and have enough down to be able to survive a night without help. Sometimes the parent bird stays away for a while after humans have visited it.

A city roof can be the perfect site for a hack box.

# Big City Homes

Peregrine falcons have been released successfully from hack boxes in many North American cities.

Cities offer peregrines plenty of small birds to feed on and lots of high-up nesting ledges.

# Falconers Saving Falcons

**F**alconry is a sport in which people train falcons to hunt and fly back to them with their prey. The sport began in China more than 3,000 years ago, and is still practised in many countries.

Young peregrines have a tough time surviving their first year in the wild. Many Canadian falconers, therefore, volunteer to fly young peregrines to help them survive.

The University of Saskatchewan matches young peregrines with falconers, who fly the birds every day for at least a year. Daily exercise strengthens the birds and gives them hunting practice while they are under the falconers' care.

This expert hunter is three years old and ready to raise its own family.

# What Can You Do?

Find out as much as possible about all endangered species and what is being done to help them. Then tell others what you have learned. Try these sources:

**1.** Your school and public libraries.

**2.** National Wildlife Federation, Correspondence Division, 1400 16th St. N.W., Washington D.C. 20036.

**3.** U.S Fish and Wildlife Service, 4401 N. Fairfax Drive, Room 130, Arlington, VA 22203 (for information on peregrine falcons).

Get involved in helping the environment. Take part in OWL and *Chickadee* Magazines' HOOT Club Awards Program. Write to OWL Magazine, 255 Great Arrow Avenue, Buffalo N.Y. 14207-3082.

Answers to Quiz
1-b, 2-c, 3-b, 4-a, 5-c, 6-c, 7-b